MY FIRST

PARTY

B·O·O·K

ANGELA WILKES

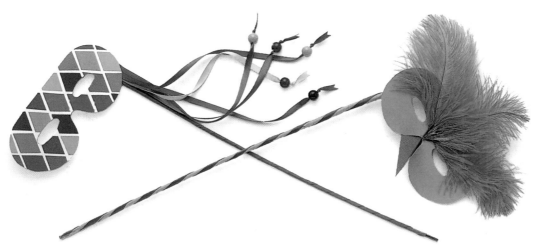

DORLING KINDERSLEY • LONDON

A Dorling Kindersley book

For Florence

Design Mathewson Bull

Photography Dave King

Home Economist Dolly Meers

Editor Marie Greenwood

Art Director Roger Priddy

First published in Great Britain in 1991 by
Dorling Kindersley Limited,
9 Henrietta Street, London WC2E 8PS

**A CIP catalogue record for this book
is available from the British Library**

Colour reproduction by Colorscan, Singapore
Printed in Italy by LEGO

Dorling Kindersley would like to thank Jonathan Buckley,
Sarah Cole, Mahreen Khan and Sarah Kramer for their help
in producing this book.

Illustrations by Brian Delf

CONTENTS

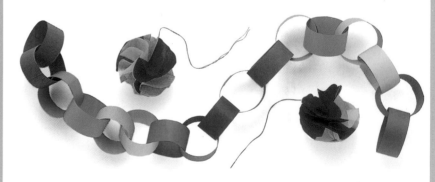

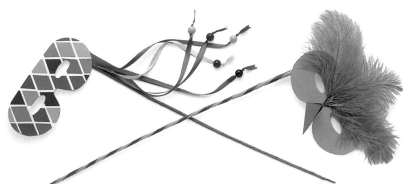

A PICTURE GUIDE TO PARTIES

My First Party Book shows you how to get ready for a party. There are delicious things to cook and clever ideas for things to make. Simple step-by-step instructions show you exactly what to do and there are life-size photographs of the finished projects. On the opposite page is a list of things to read before you start and below are the points to look for in each project.

How to use this book

Equipment
These illustrated checklists show you which utensils or equipment you need to have ready before you start.

The things you need
The ingredients or materials for each project are shown life-size, to help you check you have everything you need.

Step-by-step
Step-by-step photographs and clear instructions show you what to do at each stage of the recipe or project.

MAKING DIPS

Dips are one of the easiest and tastiest things to eat at a party. Make a selection of dips, provide lots of things to dunk into them and leave your guests to help themselves. Here are the ingredients for a simple basic dip, plus different things to add to it to vary the flavour. On the next two pages you will find some unusual ideas on how to decorate the dips and make them a fun addition to any party table.

You will need

For the basic dip

EQUIPMENT

2 bowls   Chopping board

Knife   Wooden spoon

Fork   Spoon

3 tablespoons yogurt or mayonnaise

225g (8oz) cream or curd cheese

For the chunky dip

198g (7oz) cooked sweetcorn

For the avocado dip

Half a lemon   *1 avocado*

For the peanut butter dip

Half a red pepper

Chives

3 tablespoons peanut butter

For the tuna dip

198 g (7 oz) tinned tuna fish

The basic dip
Put the cream cheese in a mixing bowl. Mash it with a fork until it is smooth and creamy, then stir in the yogurt or mayonnaise.

Chunky dip
Deseed the pepper and cut it into small chunks. Chop the chives finely. Stir the chives, pepper and sweetcorn into the basic dip.

Peanut butter dip
Add the peanut butter to the basic dip mixture, a spoonful at a time, and stir everything together well.

Tuna dip
Use mayonnaise rather than yogurt to make the basic dip. Drain the tuna fish, mash it up with a fork and stir it into the dip mixture.

Avocado dip
1 Cut the avocado in half and dig out the stone with a spoon. Scoop the flesh of the avocado into a bowl.

2 Squeeze the juice of the lemon into the bowl. Mash the avocado with a fork, then add the basic dip mixture to it and stir well.

20

21

4

Things to remember

1 Do not cook anything unless there is an adult there to help you.

2 Read the instructions before you start, to make sure you have everything you need.

3 Wash your hands and put on an apron or old shirt before you start.

4 Carefully weigh or measure all the ingredients you use before cooking.

5 Always wear oven gloves when picking up hot dishes, or when putting things into or taking them out of the oven.

6 Be very careful with sharp knives and scissors. **Do not use them unless an adult is there to help you.**

7 Never leave the oven while electric or gas rings are turned on. Always turn the oven off when you have finished cooking.

8 When you have finished, wash up, put everything away, and clean up any mess.

Decoration
These pictures show the ingredients or materials you need to decorate the things you have made.

The final results
Life-size pictures show you what the finished projects look like, making it easy for you to copy them.

The oven glove symbol
Whenever you see this symbol by a picture or instruction, it means that you should ask an adult for help.

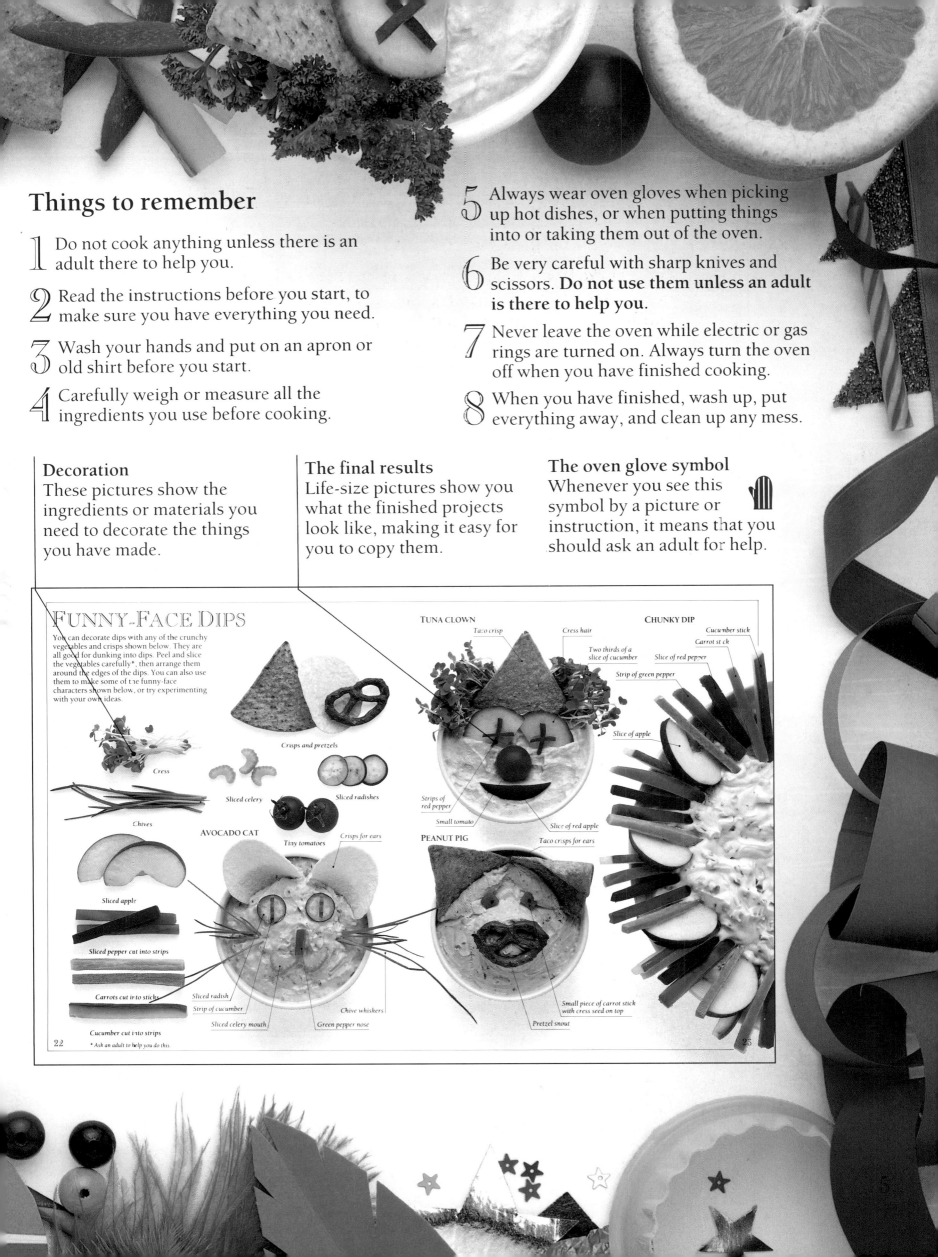

FUNNY-FACE DIPS

You can decorate dips with any of the crunchy vegetables and crisps shown below. They are all good for dunking into dips. Peel and slice the vegetables carefully*, then arrange them around the edges of the dips. You can also use them to make some of the funny-face characters shown below, or try experimenting with your own ideas.

Cress

Chives

Sliced apple

Sliced pepper cut into strips

Carrots cut into sticks

Cucumber cut into strips

Crisps and pretzels

Sliced celery

Sliced radishes

Tiny tomatoes

AVOCADO CAT

Crisps for ears

Sliced radish
Strip of cucumber
Sliced celery mouth

Chive whiskers
Green pepper nose

TUNA CLOWN

Taco crisp

Cress hair

Two thirds of a slice of cucumber

Strips of red pepper

Small tomato

Slice of red apple

PEANUT PIG

Taco crisps for ears

Small piece of carrot stick with cress seed on top

Pretzel snout

CHUNKY DIP

Cucumber stick

Carrot stick

Slice of red pepper

Strip of green pepper

Slice of apple

22   * Ask an adult to help you do this

23

PARTY INVITATIONS

The first thing you will need to do is make the party invitations. Home-made invitations are much more fun than shop ones and you can make them fit the theme of the party. Here we show you how to make three different kinds of invitation. Turn the page to see what they will look like when they are finished and to find out what to write on them.

Thin card

Small sequins

You will need

EQUIPMENT

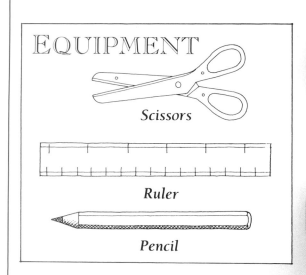

Scissors

Ruler

Pencil

Glitter

A glue stick

Coloured ribbons

Coloured paper

Coloured foil

6

Cut-out invitations

Draw the shapes you want on thin card, or copy the Easter egg or Christmas tree on pages 8 and 9. Cut the shapes out of the card.

Christmas tree invitation

Glue coloured foil on to the tree's pot. Spread glue over the tree and sprinkle green glitter over it. Glue sequins on to the glitter.

Easter egg invitation

Cut out strips of coloured paper. Cut some strips into triangles. Copying the picture on page 9, glue the shapes to the egg card.

Concertina invitation

1 Cut out a piece of paper 50 cm by 8.5 cm. Make a fold 7 cm from one end of it, then fold the paper every 7 cm, to pleat it.

2 Draw a person on the top fold of paper. Its feet and legs must go over the sides of the paper. Cut around the person.

3 Open the paper out. You will have a row of people. Make a folded card. Glue the person at the end inside the card on the left side.

Animal invitation

1 Draw large animals or dinosaurs on coloured card. You can copy the crocodile and dinosaur on pages 8 and 9.

2 Copying the cards overleaf, cut scales, claws and eyes out of coloured paper. Glue them to the crocodile and dinosaur cards.

3 Cut out the cards. Fold each one in half widthways, then in half again. There should be three folds down each card.

Turn the page to see how to add the finishing touches to your party invitations.

COME TO MY PARTY

And here are the finished invitations! Write the details of your party on the backs of the Christmas tree, Easter egg, and dinosaur invitations, and on the cards with the crocodile and the row of little people.

On each invitation write the name of the person you are inviting, then your name, the date and time of the party and your address. If you want a reply to the invitation, write R.S.V.P.* at the bottom of it.

GLITTERING TREE

Make a hole in the top of each invitation and tie a narrow ribbon through it, so that your friends can hang them from their Christmas tree at home.

Coloured paper scales

Small sequins

Green glitter

Coloured paper claws

GREEN CROCODILE

Shiny red foil

HOLDING HANDS INVITATION

Concertina row of little people

Please come to Emma's party on 4th May at 3 p.m. at 3 Cedar Road R.S.V.P.

Small card decorated with pieces of coloured card

STEGOSAURUS

Strips of coloured paper

EASTER EGG

Triangles of coloured paper

Ribbon tied in a bow for decoration

White card glued to jaws

Coloured paper eye

Eye made of coloured paper

To Sam

* This means "Please reply".

9

MAKING DECORATIONS

Decorating the room where you are going to have your party is great fun, especially if you ask some friends to help you. Arm yourself with a few packets of crêpe and tissue paper and within no time at all you can magic up rainbow-coloured paper chains, giant streamers and multi-coloured pompoms. Turn the page to see the dramatic results.

Crêpe paper

You will need

Coloured paper

A glue stick

Thread (for the pompoms)

Tissue paper

Sticky tape

EQUIPMENT

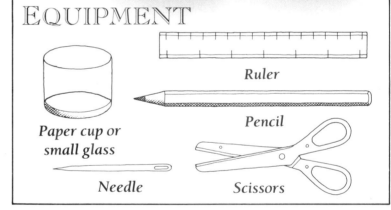

Paper cup or small glass

Ruler

Pencil

Needle

Scissors

Streamers

1 Cut two long strips of crêpe paper the same width, keeping the paper folded. Snip along the edges of the strips to fringe them.

2 Tape the strips of paper together at one end. Twist them together all the way along. Tape the other ends together.

10

Rainbow chains

1 Cut coloured paper or crêpe paper into long strips about 2.5 cm wide. For a rainbow chain, use lots of different colours.

2 Cut each strip into pieces about 18 cm long. Roll a piece of paper into a ring, as shown, and glue down the outer edge.

3 Loop another piece of paper through the ring and glue it. Keep on doing this until the chain is the length you want.

Plaited chain

1 Cut two long strips of crêpe paper the same width in different colours*. Tape the two ends together, as shown.

2 Fold the bottom strip of paper across the top strip. Then fold the new bottom strip of paper up over the strip of paper on top.

3 Carry on plaiting the two strips of paper together. Tape the ends together. Then gently pull the ends of the chain apart.

Tissue paper pompoms

1 Draw circles on folded coloured tissue paper, by drawing around a paper cup or glass. Cut out the circles of paper.

2 Fold eight circles of tissue paper into quarters. Thread the point of each one on to a knotted piece of thread.

3 Do two small stitches in the tissue paper and cut the thread, leaving a loose end. Open out each circle of paper.

Leave the paper folded, as in the packet, when you cut it. 11

DASHING DECORATIONS

Tape the paper chains and streamers to the walls of your party room, or loop them around fireplaces, doorways, mirrors, or pictures (ask your parents first). Hang or tape groups of tissue paper pompoms in the joins between two streamers or chains. Your room will be full of colour, ready for the party to begin.

CRÊPE PAPER CHAIN

RAINBOW CHAIN

PLAITED CHAIN

12

CRÊPE PAPER STREAMER

TISSUE PAPER POMPOMS

13

PUNCHES AND SHAKES

With the simplest of ingredients you can create wonderful drinks for your party. Below you can find out how to make a basic fruit punch and milk shake and over the page there are recipes for five mouthwatering cocktails on the same theme.

Drinking-chocolate powder

Frozen raspberries

You will need

Blackcurrant syrup

Honey

Plain yogurt

Orange juice

Lemonade

Vanilla ice cream

Milk

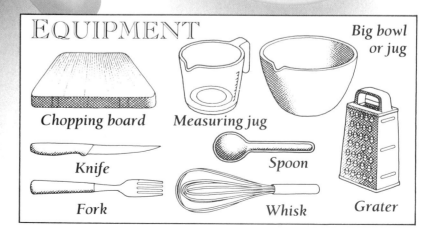

EQUIPMENT

Big bowl or jug

Chopping board   Measuring jug

Knife   Spoon

Fork   Whisk   Grater

A banana

For decoration

Sliced fruit

Grated chocolate

Making a fruit punch

1 Wash the fruit you are going to use. Cut it into halves and take out any stones or pips, then slice the fruit finely.

2 Put the fruit into a big bowl or jug. Pour fruit juice, or syrup, and lemonade over the fruit and gently stir everything together.

Making a milk shake

1 Prepare the fruit you are going to use. Peel and slice bananas. Take frozen fruit out of the freezer and allow time to defrost.

2 Put the fruit in a big bowl and mash it with a fork. You can use a blender to mash the fruit if there is an adult to help you.

3 Add the other ingredients (as listed in the recipes for the drinks on the next page). Mix everything together well.

15

PARTY COCKTAILS

And here are five delicious fruit punches and milk shakes based on the recipes shown on the last two pages. Serve them in tall glasses or paper cups and decorate them with sliced fruit and grated chocolate. All the quantities given make drinks for two people, so increase the quantities as necessary.

RASPBERRY FROTH
4 tablespoons raspberries
2 cups milk
2 tablespoons vanilla ice cream
4 teaspoons honey

Follow the milk shake recipe and decorate with a few raspberries.

ORANGES AND LEMONS
1 cup of orange juice
1 cup of lemonade

Make this like a fruit punch, then slot halved slices of orange around the edge of the glass.

BANANA DREAM
½ cup milk
½ cup yogurt
2 tablespoons vanilla ice cream
1 banana
1 teaspoon honey

Follow the milk shake recipe on page 15 to make the banana dream. Decorate it with slices of banana and kiwi fruit threaded on to a straw.

RUBY FRUIT PUNCH

2 tablespoons blackcurrant
juice
2 cups lemonade
Sliced apple and nectarine

*Follow the punch recipe to
make the ruby fruit punch.*

CHOCO SHAKE

1 tablespoon chocolate
powder
2 cups of milk
Grated chocolate

*Follow the milk shake recipe,
but mix the chocolate powder
with a little hot water before
adding the milk. Sprinkle the
finished drink with grated
chocolate.*

PICTURE STRAWS

You can give your party drinks a personal touch by making a special picture straw for each of your guests. Try painting simple animal faces, flags, or flowers, like those shown on the opposite page, or experiment with some ideas of your own. Write the name of each guest on the back of the picture cards to make them into place names for your party table.

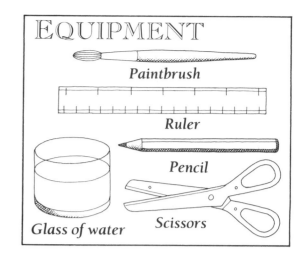

EQUIPMENT

Paintbrush

Ruler

Pencil

Glass of water   Scissors

You will need

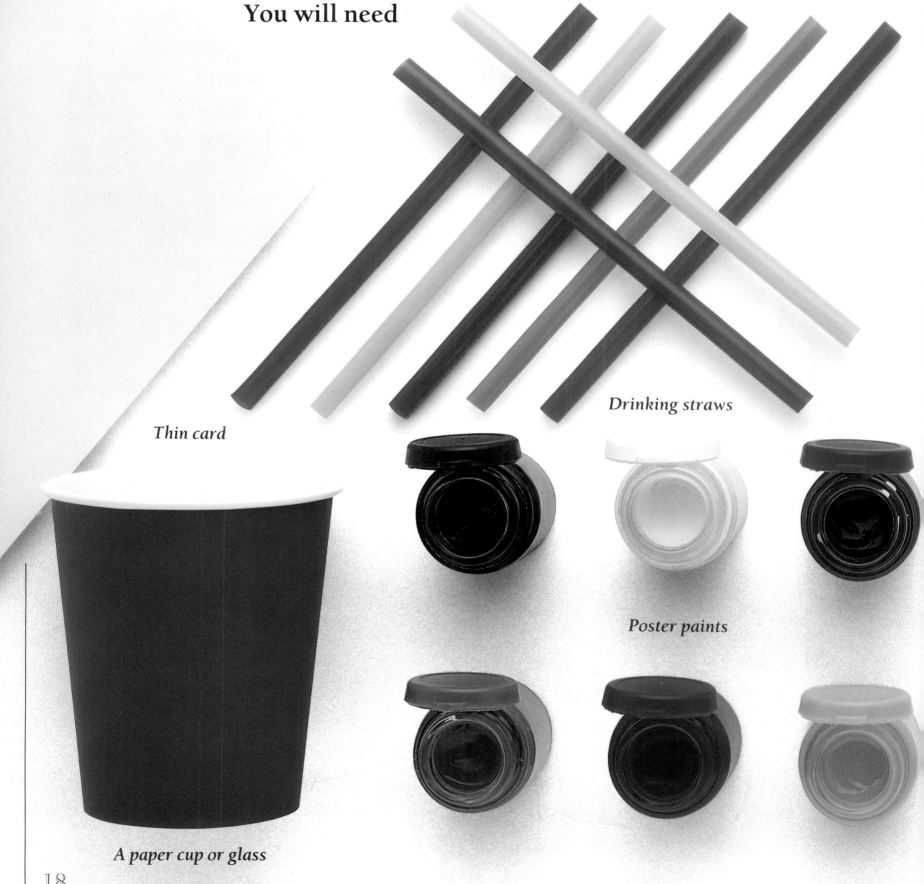

Drinking straws

Thin card

Poster paints

A paper cup or glass

What to do

1 Draw circles on the card, by drawing around the base of the paper cup or glass. If you want to make flags, draw rectangles.

2 Draw an animal face or flower on each circle, then add ears or other details. Paint them. Paint a flag on each rectangle.

3 Cut out the pictures. Using the point of your scissors, cut small slits near the top and bottom of each picture, as shown*.

Finishing the straws

4 Carefully push a straw into the bottom slit of each picture, and then back out again through the top slit. Animal faces work best if the bottom slit is cut along the mouth.

FLAG

POPPY

COCKEREL

CAT

PANDA

* Ask an adult to help you do this.

19

Making Dips

Dips are one of the easiest and tastiest things to eat at a party. Make a selection of dips, provide lots of things to dunk into them and leave your guests to help themselves. Here are the ingredients for a simple basic dip, plus different things to add to it to vary the flavour. On the next two pages you will find some unusual ideas on how to decorate the dips and make them a fun addition to any party table.

You will need

For the basic dip

3 tablespoons yogurt or mayonnaise

EQUIPMENT

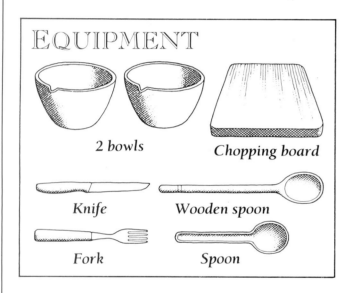

2 bowls

Chopping board

Knife

Wooden spoon

Fork

Spoon

200 g (8 oz) cream or curd cheese

The basic dip

Put the cream cheese in a mixing bowl. Mash it with a fork until it is smooth and creamy, then stir in the yogurt or mayonnaise.

Chunky dip

Deseed the pepper and cut it into small chunks. Chop the chives finely. Stir the chives, pepper and sweetcorn into the basic dip.

Peanut butter dip

Add the peanut butter to the basic dip mixture, a spoonful at a time, and stir everything together well.

For the chunky dip

For the peanut butter dip

Half a red pepper

Chives

175 g (7 oz) cooked sweetcorn

3 tablespoons peanut butter

For the avocado dip

For the tuna dip

Half a lemon

1 avocado

175 g (7 oz) tinned tuna fish

Tuna dip

Avocado dip

Use mayonnaise rather than yogurt to make the basic dip. Drain the tuna fish, mash it up with a fork and stir it into the dip mixture.

1 Cut the avocado in half and dig out the stone with a spoon. Scoop the flesh of the avocado into a bowl.

2 Squeeze the juice of the lemon into the bowl. Mash the avocado with a fork, then add the basic dip mixture to it and stir well.

FUNNY-FACE DIPS

You can decorate dips with any of the crunchy vegetables and crisps shown below. They are all good for dunking into dips. Peel and slice the vegetables carefully*, then arrange them around the edges of the dips. You can also use them to make some of the funny-face characters shown below, or try experimenting with your own ideas.

Crisps and pretzels

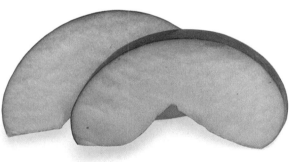

Cress

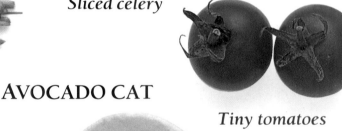

Sliced celery

Sliced radishes

Chives

AVOCADO CAT

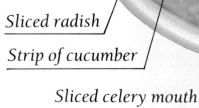

Tiny tomatoes

Crisps for ears

Sliced apple

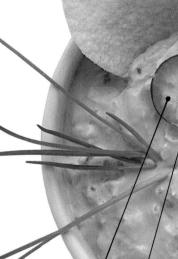

Sliced pepper cut into strips

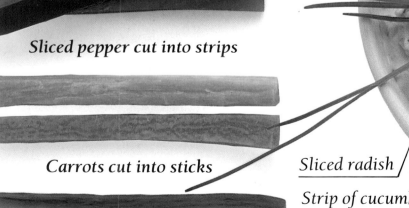

Carrots cut into sticks

Chive whiskers

Sliced radish

Strip of cucumber

Sliced celery mouth

Green pepper nose

Cucumber cut into strips

* Ask an adult to help you do this.

TUNA CLOWN

Taco crisp

Cress hair

Two thirds of a slice of cucumber

Strips of red pepper

Small tomato

Slice of red apple

CHUNKY DIP

Cucumber stick

Carrot stick

Slice of red pepper

Strip of green pepper

Slice of apple

PEANUT PIG

Taco crisps for ears

Small piece of carrot stick with cress seed on top

Pretzel snout

23

MYSTERY MASKS

Give your party a touch of mystery by asking all your guests to wear masks. Here you can find out how to make three festive carnival masks from one basic mask pattern, by using different coloured paper and adding sparkling glitter and swirling ribbons. Turn the page to see the finished magical disguises. Even your best friend won't recognise you!

You will need

Sticky tape

A glue stick

Garden sticks

Gold gift tape

Beads

Gummed stars

Glitter

Coloured paper

Tracing paper

Thin card

Mask pattern

Ribbons

Feathers

Making the basic mask

1 Trace the mask pattern on the opposite page on to tracing paper. Don't forget to trace the eyes as well as the outline.

2 Turn the tracing over. Lay it on card and scribble over the traced lines, to transfer them to the card. Cut out the mask*.

Harlequin mask

1 Using the picture of the mask on page 27 as a guide, cut out 25 diamonds of coloured paper all the same size.

2 Glue the diamond shapes to the mask in rows, leaving a little space around each one. Trim the ones that cover the eye holes.

3 Tape five ribbons of the same length to the back of the mask at one side. Thread a bead on to each ribbon and tie a knot below.

4 Wind ribbon all the way down a garden stick. Tape the ends of the ribbon down. Tape the stick to the back of the mask.

* Ask an adult to help you do this.

25

FESTIVE FACES

Glitter mask

1 Spread glue over a card mask and sprinkle green glitter on top. Sprinkle red glitter around the edge of the mask and the eyes.

2 Glue on a few shiny gummed stars for decoration. Glue a feather to the mask above the outer edge of one eye.

3 Wind gold gift tape all the way down a garden stick. Tape the two ends down. Tape the stick to the back of the mask, to one side.

Bird of Paradise mask

1 Trace and cut out a mask in orange paper, as well as one in card. Glue the orange paper mask to the card mask.

2 Glue a feather to the centre of the mask, pointing upwards. Glue on two more feathers so they fan out on either side of it.

3 Cut out a triangle of blue paper 12 cm long and 5 cm wide at the top. Fold it in half and make a slit at the top of the fold.

4 Fold back a flap on either side of the slit. Glue the flaps to the centre back of the mask to make the beak point out in front.

5 Cover a garden stick with strips of orange paper. Wind ribbon over the top of it. Tape the stick to the back of the mask.

GLITTER MASK

HARLEQUIN MASK

BIRD OF PARADISE MASK

27

MAKING SANDWICHES

With a little imagination, simple sandwiches can be transformed into a real party-time treat. Here you can find out how to make different types of sandwich and filling, and over the page you can see how to decorate and arrange them to create all kinds of picture sandwiches.

Sandwich fillings

Chopped hard-boiled eggs mixed with mayonnaise

You will need

Butter

Sliced cheese

Grated cheese and carrot mixed with mayonnaise

Slices of ham

Small bread rolls

Mashed tuna fish and mayonnaise

Sliced dark brown, light brown, and white bread

Chopped, cooked chicken and mayonnaise

Cream cheese

EQUIPMENT

Biscuit cutters

Grater

Fork

Knife

Cocktail sticks

Cling film or tin foil

Chopping board

For decoration

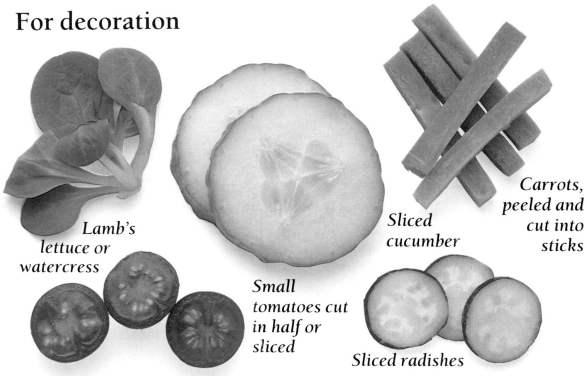

Lamb's lettuce or watercress

Small tomatoes cut in half or sliced

Sliced cucumber

Sliced radishes

Carrots, peeled and cut into sticks

Filled rolls

Make two cuts in each roll. Fill the top cut with sandwich filling. Arrange cucumber, tomato or radishes in the bottom cut.

Galleon rolls

Cut rolls in half. Spread them with butter and sandwich filling. Make sails from triangles of sliced cheese on cocktail sticks*.

Patchwork sandwiches

Make sandwiches with sliced dark brown and white bread. Trim off the crusts. Cut the sandwiches into small squares the same size.

Shaped sandwiches

Butter slices of bread. Cut shapes out of them with biscuit cutters. Cut the same shapes out of sliced cheese and lay them on the bread.

Pinwheel sandwiches

1 Trim the crusts off sliced white bread. Spread each slice of bread with cream cheese and lay a slice of ham on top.

2 Roll the slices of bread up lengthways and wrap them tightly in cling film or tin foil. Put them in the fridge to chill.

3 After two hours, take the rolls out of the fridge. Unwrap them and cut them into slices about 1 cm thick.

* Be careful with cocktail sticks as they have sharp points.   *Turn the page to see how to decorate and arrange the sandwiches.*   29

SANDWICH BONANZA

And here are the finished sandwiches and rolls with some ideas on how to lay them out on your party table. Arrange small filled rolls to look like a hungry caterpillar wiggling across a plate, complete with legs and antennae. Scatter animal sandwiches on a meadow made from shredded lettuce, and create a patchwork quilt of tiny brown and white sandwiches. Your hungry guests will not know what to eat first!

Cheese and carrot filling

Antennae made from tiny tomatoes on cocktail sticks

MUNCHING CATERPILLAR

Watercress or lamb's lettuce

BUTTERFLY SANDWICH

Cress

Sliced tomato and cucumber

GALLEON ROLLS

Strip of tomato

Sliced radishes

Sail made from slice of cheese on cocktail stick

Shredded lettuce

CHEESY PIG SANDWICHES

Egg mayonnaise filling

Legs made from
carrot sticks

Chicken filling

Sliced radishes

Tuna fish filling

Sliced tomato and cucumber

Chicken filling

Sliced radish
and cucumber

Cheese and
carrot filling

**PINWHEEL
SANDWICHES**

**PATCHWORK
SANDWICHES**

Sandwich made with
white bread

Dark brown bread sandwich

31

BUTTERY BISCUITS

Homemade biscuits are quick and easy to make and taste far better than any you buy. Below is a recipe for delicious, buttery shortbread biscuits. You can make plain biscuits, lemon ones or chocolate ones. The ingredients shown will make 15-20 biscuits, depending on the size of your biscuit cutters. Turn the page for ideas on how to decorate your biscuits.

You will need

50 g (2 oz) caster sugar

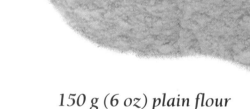

100 g (4 oz) softened butter

150 g (6 oz) plain flour

What to do

1 Set the oven at 170°C/325°F/ Gas Mark 3. Rub butter all over the baking tray so that the biscuits will not stick to it.

2 Put the butter and sugar in the mixing bowl. Beat together with a wooden spoon until the mixture is soft and creamy.

3 Sift the flour. Add the cocoa powder or lemon rind if wished. Mix, then make a ball of dough with your hands*.

* If the mixture seems too crumbly, add a teaspoon or two of water.

EQUIPMENT

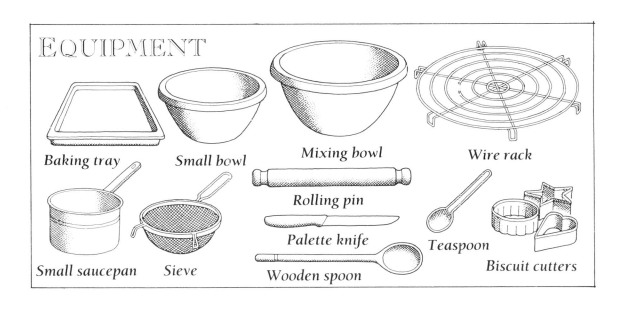

Baking tray   Small bowl   Mixing bowl   Wire rack

Rolling pin

Palette knife   Teaspoon

Small saucepan   Sieve   Wooden spoon   Biscuit cutters

For chocolate biscuits

25 g (1 oz) cocoa powder to replace 25 g (1 oz) of the flour you use.

For lemon biscuits

2 teaspoons finely grated lemon rind

4 Sprinkle flour on a table and your rolling pin. Roll out the dough until about 5 mm thick. Press with your hands if it cracks.

5 Cut the dough into shapes and lift them on to the baking tray. Gather up any scraps of dough left and roll them out again.

6 You can decorate some biscuits now (see over the page). Bake for 15-20 minutes, then place on a wire rack to cool.

SWEET TREATS

You can decorate biscuits before they are cooked by pressing chopped nuts, cherries or Hundreds and thousands into the dough. Or you can cook the biscuits, then coat or dip them in melted chocolate before decorating them.

Brown chocolate

White chocolate

For decoration you will need

Walnuts

Glacé cherries

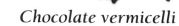

Smarties

Chocolate covering

Chocolate vermicelli

Hundreds and thousands

1 Break the chocolate up into a bowl*. Heat some water in a saucepan over a low heat until it just begins to bubble.

2 Stand the bowl over the saucepan over a low heat. Gently stir the chocolate with a wooden spoon until it has melted.

3 When the biscuits are cool, dip them in the chocolate or spoon chocolate on to them and spread it out with a knife.

NUTTY BISCUITS

CHERRY COOKIES

Biscuits decorated with chopped walnuts before being baked.

Biscuits with chopped glacé cherries pressed into them.

AEROPLANE BISCUITS
White chocolate sprinkled with Hundreds and thousands.

Brown chocolate sprinkled with chocolate vermicelli.

FINGER BISCUITS
Bar-shaped plain and chocolate biscuits with each end dipped in melted chocolate.

HEART BISCUIT

Hundreds and thousands

DOG AND CAT BISCUITS
Eye made from dot of melted chocolate

Paws dipped in melted chocolate

Chocolate biscuit dipped in white chocolate

FAIRY STAR

TRAFFIC LIGHT

CHOCOLATE STAR

Circle of melted white chocolate on a chocolate flavoured biscuit. Smartie centre

Hundreds and thousands

Melted chocolate

Smarties

* If using two different types of chocolate, break them into separate bowls

PARTY HATS

If you are going to a fancy dress party or a party with a theme, you can create magnificent hats with the simplest materials. Below we show you how to make a crown, a headband and a cone-shaped hat. Over the page you will find ideas on how to decorate them and on pages 40 and 41 you can see the spectacular results.

You will need

Sticky tape

Thin coloured card

A glue stick

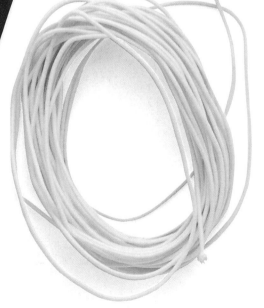

Thin elastic

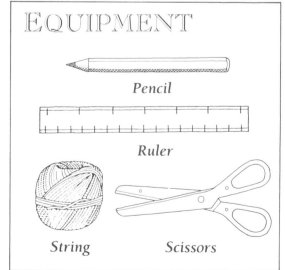

EQUIPMENT

Pencil

Ruler

String   *Scissors*

Cone hat

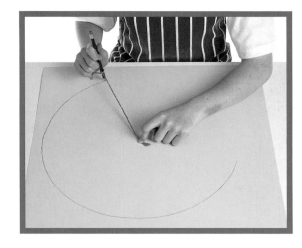

1 Draw a big circle on a sheet of card, using a pencil tied to the end of a piece of string*. Cut out the circle.

2 Cut a slit to the centre of the circle. Slide one edge of the slit over the other to make a cone. Glue down the top edge.

3 Make a hole at each side of the hat. Thread elastic with a knot at one end through the holes. Tie a knot in the other end.

Crown

1 On gold card measure out and draw a strip about 58 cm long and 6 cm deep. Carefully cut out the strip of card.

2 Cut triangles about 5 cm deep out of the top edge of the piece of card. They should all be the same size.

3 Bend the piece of card into a crown. Lap the edges over each other and tape them together inside the crown.

Headband

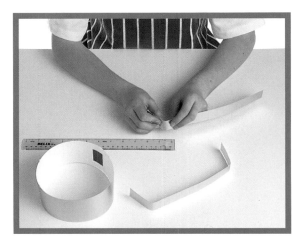

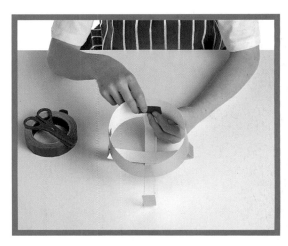

1 Cut out a piece of card about 6 cm by 60 cm. Bend the card into a band that fits your head and tape the ends, as for the crown.

2 For a crown, make a gold band. Then cut two strips of card 30 cm by 2 cm. Make folds 6 cm from the ends of the strips.

3 Tape the two strips of card to the inside of the headband, so that they cross each other above the centre of it.

Ask an adult to help you.

FANCY HATS

Here you can find out how to create five colourful hats and headdresses simply by decorating the hats you learnt how to make on pages 36 and 37 in different ways.

You will need

Purple tissue paper

Thick, coloured paper and black paper

Thin ribbons

Gold and silver paper

Shiny sweet wrappers

Cotton wool

Small round sweets

Indian headdress

1 Make a red headband. Cut out triangles the same size from different coloured paper. Glue them around the headband.

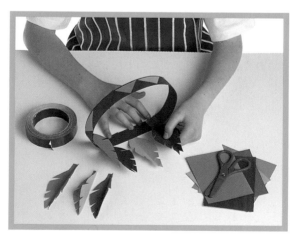

2 Cut out feathers from folded coloured paper, copying those in the picture on page 40. Tape them inside the headband.

Wizard's hat

1 Make a tall cone hat from dark blue card. Cut stars and moons out of gold and silver paper and glue them to the hat.

Crinkly shredded tissue paper

Princess's crown

1 Make a crown and glue a ribbon around its base. Cut out circles of coloured paper. Glue them to the points of the crown.

2 Cover some small sweets with shiny sweet wrappers, so they look like jewels. Glue them to the crown and the bobbles on top.

King's crown

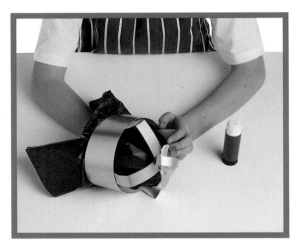

1 Make a headband-type crown. Cut out two strips of gold card about 15 cm by 1.5 cm. Glue them into two overlapping rings.

2 Glue the gold rings to the top of the crown. Push a folded piece of purple tissue paper up into the crown and glue it in place.

3 Glue cotton wool around the base of the crown. Glue on tiny pieces of black paper. Glue sweetie jewels to the crown.

Clown's hat

2 Tape some thin ribbons to the top of the hat. Tape gold and silver stars and moons to the ends of the ribbons.

1 Make a yellow cone hat. Cut out two pink paper circles and glue them to the hat. Glue small blue circles on top of them.

2 Tape a tuft of crinkly shredded tissue paper to the top of the hat and two larger tufts to the base, one at each side.

ON PARADE

These hats will transform you into the characters of your dreams! Raid the dressing-up box to find the right clothes to wear with your hat, or drape yourself in a large piece of fabric which can act as regal robes or a wizard's cloak.

CLOWN'S HAT

Circle of pink paper

Circle of blue paper glued on to circle of pink paper

Shredded tissue paper

INDIAN HEADDRESS

Feather made from coloured paper

Thin ribbons

Triangle of coloured paper

PRINCESS'S CROWN

Jewel made of sweet wrapped in sweet wrapper

Sweetie jewel

Ribbon

KING'S CROWN

Rings made from gold card

Sweetie jewel

Purple tissue paper

Fur made from cotton wool

WIZARD'S HAT

Small pieces of black paper

Moons and stars cut out of gold and silver paper

SPECIAL CHOCOLATE CAKE

You will need

The most important feature of any party food is the cake, so here is a recipe for a moist, dark chocolate cake that can take pride of place on the table. The quantities given below are enough to make one 18 cm sandwich cake and about 12 buns, some of which you will need for the cake. Turn the page to see how to ice and decorate the cake in a very special way.

3 tablespoons cocoa powder

EQUIPMENT

Pastry brush

2 non-stick 18 cm (7 in) shallow cake tins

2 mixing bowls

Teaspoon

Sieve

A bun tin or individual tins

Fork or whisk

Wire rack

Palette knife

Wooden spoon

225 g (9 oz) plain flour

Making the cake

1 Set the oven at 180°C/325°F/ Gas Mark 3. Brush some oil around the insides of the two cake tins and the bun tin.

2 Sift the flour, baking powder, cocoa powder, bicarbonate of soda and sugar into one mixing bowl. Mix together well.

3 Break the eggs into another bowl and beat them well. Add the treacle, vegetable oil and milk and whisk everything together.

175 g (7 oz)
caster sugar

225 ml (3/8 pt)
warm milk

3 medium eggs, beaten

225 ml (3/8 pt)
vegetable oil

1 1/2 teaspoons baking powder

1 1/2 teaspoons
bicarbonate of soda

3 tablespoons black treacle

4 Make a hollow in the flour mixture. Pour the egg and treacle mixture into the hollow and stir everything together well.

5 Pour about a third of the cake mixture into each sandwich tin and smooth it level. Pour the rest into the bun tin.

6 Bake the cakes for 20-25 minutes and the buns for 10-15 minutes, until they feel springy. Put them on a wire rack to cool.

THE BIRTHDAY CAKE

The finished chocolate cake is filled and iced with chocolate butter icing. The sides of the cake are coated in grated chocolate. Follow the instructions below to find out what to do, then copy the picture on the opposite page to decorate the cake and transform it into a charming funny-face bear.

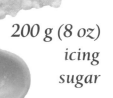

You will need

200 g (8 oz) softened butter

1 tablespoon cocoa powder

200 g (8 oz) icing sugar

2 tablespoons jam

Icing the cake

1 Beat the butter in a bowl until soft and creamy. Sift in the icing sugar and cocoa powder. Add a little water and mix well.

2 Spread a third of the icing on one cake. Put the other cake on top and spread another third of the icing over it.

3 Spread a thin layer of jam all around the sides of the cake. Carefully pat on grated chocolate until the sides are covered.

4 Use four buns for the bear's ears. Ice them and coat the sides with jam and grated chocolate, as with the big cake.

Grated brown and white chocolate

Things for decoration

Chopped nuts

Brown and white chocolate buttons

Licorice sweets

Chocolate buttons

Two dark Smarties

A glacé cherry

Cut off a third of each iced bun. Stick them to the cake with icing, to make the bear's ears

The finished cake

Eyebrows made of licorice sweets

Eyes made of white chocolate buttons and dark brown Smarties

Licorice sweets

Muzzle made of chopped nuts

Chocolate button cheeks

Grated chocolate

Glacé cherry

45

CHOCOLATE MEDALS

What better for the winners of your party games than gleaming medals on shiny ribbons, each one concealing a disc of delicious chocolate? Below you can see how to make the medals. You can make them out of brown or white chocolate, or both. If you use more than one kind of chocolate, melt each colour in a separate bowl, so that the colours do not mix. Turn the page to see the finished medals.

Coloured ribbons

You will need

Large bars of chocolate

Sticky tape

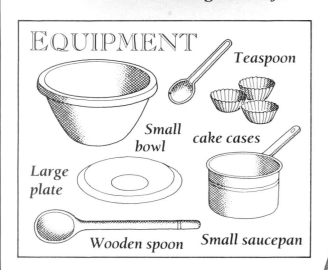

EQUIPMENT

Teaspoon

Small bowl

cake cases

Large plate

Wooden spoon

Small saucepan

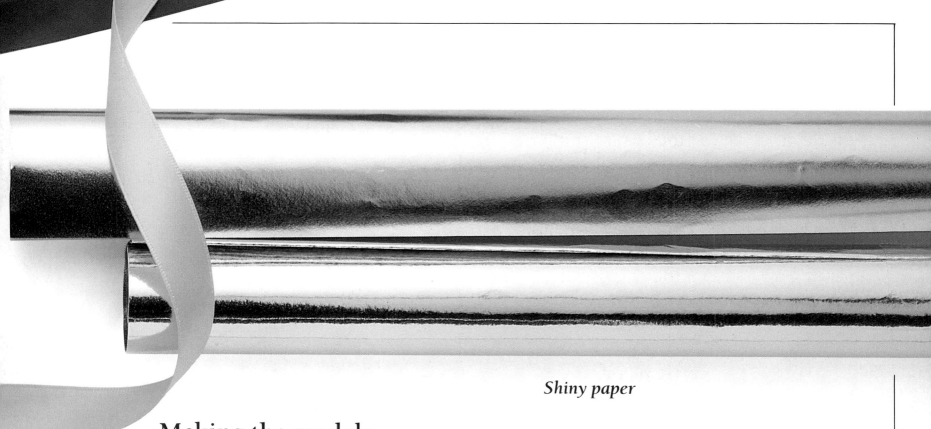

Shiny paper

Making the medals

1 Break the chocolate up into a bowl. Heat some water in the small saucepan over a low heat until it just begins to bubble.

2 Stand the bowl over the saucepan over a low heat. Stir the chocolate with a wooden spoon until it melts and is smooth.

3 Put the cake cases on a plate. Pour about ½ cm of melted chocolate into each cake case. Put the plate in the fridge.

4 Leave the chocolate discs in the fridge until they have set hard. Then gently push them up out of the paper cases.

5 Cut out squares of shiny paper. Wrap each medal in shiny paper, taping it down at the back of the medal with sticky tape.

6 Cut a piece of ribbon 70 cm long for each medal. Bend each piece of ribbon into a loop and tape it to the back of a medal.

MEDALS FOR WINNERS

And here are the finished medals! They will make good going-home presents. If you play games with more than one winner, use different coloured ribbons to show who has come first, second or third.

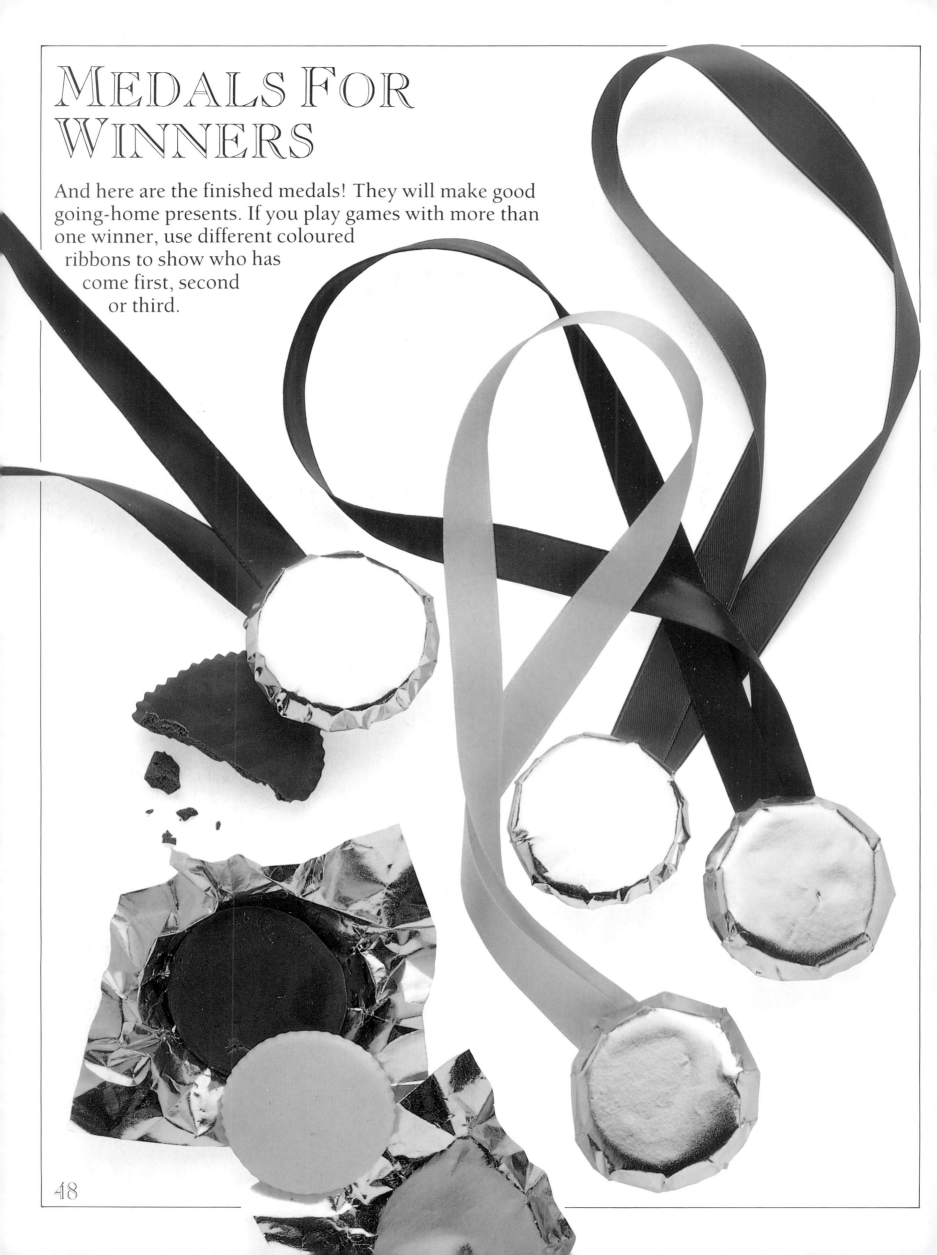